Karmic debts
Treaty of karmic numerology

Jean Marc Vignolo

From the same author in french :

- Le guide pratique des tables d'interprétation numérologique
- S'initier et se perfectionner en numérologie
- Les énergies inter-nombre
- Le jour de naissance
- Le chemin de vie
- Le guide pratique des méthodes de numérologie
- Vos années personnelles

Legal Deposit : mars 2019
ISBN : 978-2-9555064-9-3
Copyright 2019 : Jean Marc Vignolo
Cover graphic : Jean Marc Vignolo
All rights reserved

www.numerologueconseils.com

Contents

Introduction :

Karmic debts, soul, karma

Analysis, interpretation and explanation of karmic debts :

The major karmic debt 13
The intensity of the energies in the grid of inclusion
The major karmic debt 14
The intensity of the energies in the grid of inclusion
The major karmic debt 16
The intensity of the energies in the grid of inclusion
The major karmic debt 19
The intensity of the energies in the grid of inclusion
The minor karmic debt 11
The intensity of the energies in the grid of inclusion
The minor karmic debt 12
The intensity of the energies in the grid of inclusion
The minor karmic debt 15
The intensity of the energies in the grid of inclusion
The minor karmic debt 18
The intensity of the energies in the grid of inclusion
The minor karmic debt 26

Karmic accumulation :

Karmic accumulation of lessons
Karmic accumulation of major debts
Karmic accumulation of minor debts

Karmic analysis from concrete examples :

Karmic letters
Karmic days of birth

Full and detailed case study :

The dominants of the theme
The analysis of karmic debts in the identity
The inclusion grid or intensity table
The intensity of karmic debts

Karma in the cycles of life and annual:

Life Path Cycle Table
Tables of annual cycles

Other examples :

Some additional information and examples

Tables of interpretations :

Interpretation and rebalancing of karmic accumulation in lessons
Interpretation and rebalancing of karmic accumulation at the level of major and minor debts
Interpretation and rebalancing of karmic lessons
The challenges of the path of life
The foundation of numbers

Introduction

While reading this book, stay objective and take the necessary distance.
Karma is a vast subject, fascinating and fascinating to many people.
I will therefore approach Karma through karmic debts, which we use in numerology, interpret them, use them, and especially try to understand them better by analyzing them in detail, examples to support.

Karmic debts, as well as the notion of karma, are in no way connected with punishment, or any other debts to be paid, such as the bailiff coming knocking at the door to beg for his due. All action inevitably has consequences, it is the principle of cause and effect, and whatever one may say of the return of the baton is never very far. It is therefore necessary to minimize the effects of negative karma, to rebalance the vibratory energies, so that the soul can evolve favorably, it usually takes a long time, and many incarnations will be necessary for that.

In an incarnation in progress one can sometimes make a rapid rebalancing, according to the action that has been made, and if one quickly becomes aware of his error, it is still time to put the energies back to their normal equilibrium level, by having the right attitude, this to avoid burdening even more the repair work that must be done.

Whatever the subject of birth and where, or the debts to rebalance, the potential will not be the same for each of us. Some will have more advantage than others depending on their karma, personality and life path. If several people have the same debt to repair, the tests, the situations and the people will not be the same, but sometimes there may be similarities, synchronicities, in the case where two destinies intersect, or for a group of also people who have a common karma is what I call group karma or collective karma.

Collective karma does exist, whether positive or negative, for example with a sports team carrying out a common project, which can bring them to victory, or more obviously, a group of people at the same time. At the same time, at the center of an air disaster, there are of course many other examples that can support my remarks.
For me, karma is not just a negative notion that is only part of an individual's past.

I see it as an ubiquitous and evolving energy, with which we must compose, by performing negative but positive actions, hence negative and positive karma. Karma is a continuity, some negative actions of a past past, must be rebalanced, and some positive actions of a past past, are part of our achievements and our current potential.

Which means that what we do important in our present life will condition our future, and therefore at the same time, the negative actions as positive, which will influence our karma in general. The present is finally the key.

The soul before coming back or coming to earth, choosing its incarnations and the way of food on the earth plane, using the physical vehicle that will have also chosen. This vehicle which is our body, will be specific and in accordance with the destiny chosen by the soul, which includes its aspect, its physical capacities and its life span, that is why we must take care as much as possible of this loan vehicle.

For he will serve us to circulate and survey the road that the soul has assigned to us. If the road is straight and in good enough condition, a healthy body will have a good chance of arriving safely with little hindrance, if the body is weak it will also be able to do so, provided it is taken care of. but if the road is winding and crowded, the healthy body will have a much better chance of arriving at the terminus.

It is also necessary to take into account the second vehicle, which deals with the mental and spiritual part, which is none other than " **the spirit** ". A physical vehicle without a mind is like a car without a driver, there is little chance of expecting anything if the two do not work together.

The soul, in the memory of our different incarnations, knows what must be done to evolve, and to resolve the errors of the past, but it can only communicate in a certain way with the incarnate being who represents it . Through tools like numerology, tarot or any other art says, occult. Through signposts, dotting our way, these signs can take a lot of form, physical, sensitive, auditory, visual, olfactory, mental, but it is especially intuition that will be most effective, the feelings of the moment. Some people have particularly developed abilities, such as a phenomenal intuition, or proven medium abilities, which can help them progress.

I could not talk about debt and karmic numerology, without touching the soul and karma.

But in the concept of debt, what can we really see? Certainly not an unpaid, here it is not bill late to settle, but rather one or more repair that has damaged our soul and that of others, so the word debt is not really appropriate, repair and rebalancing of karmic energies yes. I will use in this book these three words.

Not should we focus on karmic debts to take the lead, as we say, the fact of just take into account its negative karma and understand it is already in itself an evolution. Things are not simple, and everyone will do their best.

The first part of the book gives you the detailed interpretation of the different karmic debts, as well as a complete exploration to better understand their true meaning, to know if they are really active or not, if they are major or minor debts, for to be able to apply them in a numerology theme.

The second part, will allow to situate them concretely and to know where one can locate a karmic debt in a theme, that with the support of some concrete examples, which will put in evidence some key positions of the personality at the level of karma.

We will also see where are the debts at the level of the different cycles of life, or of an annual theme. This book is an exploration of karmic numerology, so I will link the unavoidable inclusion grid, with karmic debts and at the same time, use the karmic lessons or missing numbers to determine the true influences of karma on one person. I would obviously talk about numbers in weakness and excess and challenges, all in relation to the key positions of the personality.

Analysis, interpretation and explanation karmic debts

There are nine karmic debts and we can find them in many parts of the theme, not just the expression, the spiritual impulse, the intimate self or the life path, but also throughout the natal and annual theme. .

It is also the annual theme that can indicate the most favorable periods for the rebalancing of a karmic debt. There are two kinds of debts, the major karmic debts which are the main, symbolized by the 13, 14, 16 and 19, and the minor karmic debts, symbolized by the 11, 12, 15, 18 and 26.

Karmic debts, are not always active, it depends on several parameters, first of all the omnipresence of a debt in a theme, its placement, whether it appears in direct or secondary reduction, and the need to check its action at the level of the inclusion grid, depending on the intensity of certain numbers, the dominant vibratory theme, represented by the most present numbers.

The 1 which is contained in each karmic debt represents us as an individual but in a negative sense, linked to actions not always glorious, according to the field where the debt is in action. Each debt thus indicates the domain, the why and the type of probable actions that have been carried out, very often to the detriment of others, but also of oneself. It is therefore not very difficult to understand how to rebalance them, it suffices to analyze the negative aspects of the numbers contained in a karmic debt and to make the comparison between each number.

Here is a very simple example with the debt 13, the 1 represents the excessive authority, with a 3 which scatters and scatters the personal energies, in the field of the 4, representing the work and the structure of life in general. If it is weak, there is dispersion and let go, inducing a lax attitude, leaving the work to others but with authority. If the 4 is strong, it is a proud attitude, obstinate and authoritarian. The explanation is succinct, but gives an idea of the negative potential of the debt.

The connection with the theme of an individual will highlight, the intensity of numbers 1, 3 and 4, to know what exactly it is.

The positive attitude is the key to success, so it is essential to understand the demands of a karmic debt, major or minor, to rebalance and repair the energies that have been abused. Any negative attitude in this incarnation will only accentuate the difficulties and increase the weight of the debt in question. The soul will have to come back again to try to repair the errors, but each time the tests risks to be even more important. It is the same thing during the present life, the unresolved situations are represented, as long as the lesson has not been understood.

Note: If a debt is not settled, the destiny will be in charge to remind you of it, by inviting you every time the same situations, and by putting you in front of your responsibilities. Each situation will bring its lot of peculiarities, its challenges and its tests to test you, and give you especially the opportunity to settle the karmic debt or the lesson in question.

It is also important to take into account the whole of a numerology theme, before drawing hasty conclusions about the different karmic debts. The study of debts is done only in the light of a complete natal chart.

Let's start with the major debts, four in number.

But before beginning the complete study of karmic debts, it is important to speak of the intensity of the vibratory energies of a theme, and especially of those which are in the inclusion. Indeed, it is from here that we will know if a debt is active or not, and if it has a major or minor influence, which means that a major debt, may, have not that a minor influence, and sometimes a minor debt can have a major influence, in some cases.

As a rule the 1 of each karmic debt, must be in strong intensity, or at least dominant for this one to be active. As the majority of debts operate on the active principle of 1, insufflant, determination, will, self-confidence, authority in excess pushing the individual to self-realization, and using the others for that, he does not would not make sense, that a karmic debt has the missing 1 in inclusion, because it would lose all its attributes pushing it to selfishness and authoritarianism. A 1 having no confidence in himself and his own abilities, can in no case be the engine of an active debt, except in the case of debt 16, or the 1 may be in weakness.

It will also be necessary to check the place and intensity of each number within the inclusion and their importance in the rest of the topic, to obtain clear and detailed information. For example, if you have in the inclusion or the theme the number 1 in strong intensity, accompanied by a 8 and a 4 also in high intensity, there is little chance that the subject can rebalance his karma, especially he has 2, 6 and 9 in weakness to the missing. In this case we have powerful yang energies and weak yin energies, any notion of empathy, understanding and sensitivity to others, are here nonexistent or little developed.

In the case where the 1, the 4 and the 8 would be powerful, but the yin energies of the 2, 6 and 9 is too, then there is possibility of rebalancing its karmas, because the yin and yang energies are also balanced, and therefore that the notions of empathy, understanding and sensitivity to others, are present.

Hence the interest of checking the balance or not between the yin and yang energies in a theme.

Karmic debts, as well as lessons and challenges are to be modulated according to each numerological theme.

Karmic debt 13: represents the domain of 4

13 = 1 + 3 = 4
Is also symbolized by the **"nameless"** arcane tarot

From my point of view, this karmic debt can affect the whole structure of life, basically it means neglecting work in a previous life, leaving others to act in its place, because of superficial attitudes that have led to dispersion of personal energies, to the detriment of others, the 1 representative, the individual and his ego, and 3 the superficiality and dispersion. Here it is the relations at the level of the work and the structure of social life in general, that this debt puts forward, the person having this karmic debt, had to show a certain laxity and a lack of implication, preferring by far , most likely focus on the pleasures of life. Hypocrisy, pride and lies can be part of it, as well as a tendency to talk too much and brag, or boast, basically to stir up the air. It can, in the case of a dominant 4, also induce an obstinate and maniacal behavior, which in no way prevents the dispersion of energies and authoritarianism.

This debt also means transformation, the end and the renewal, the constant change on the path of destiny, with the need to adapt to all these changes. It is advisable in this life to apply to the work level and to pay attention to details, especially in terms of material and life structure in general, this also includes the home and the social or social relations professional, as well as to adopt a more serious and measured attitude in behavior in general.

It also sometimes indicates for some people a fear of death that must be overcome or a special relationship with it.

The number 13 symbolizes the radical transformations without transition, sometimes unforeseen, it can affect the material and emotional plane, but also the mental and spiritual plane.

By definition the 13 induces important changes, which require rebuilding on a new, healthier basis. If the debt is particularly active, then the individual will inevitably face reversals of situation during his destiny, appearing at certain specific periods.

Like the phoenix that is reborn from its ashes, the soul will have to adapt and start again each time, as long as it does not understand the message.

If the debt is at the level of spiritual momentum :

it is the affective domain and deep desires that are concerned.

If the debt is at the expression level :

disappointments and problems in the material and professional field, but also in other areas.

If the debt is at the level of the life path :

There are risks of failure in all areas of life, and especially a lot of hardships to overcome and overcome.

In this incarnation, tests specific to this debt will be put on the path of the subject, which will have to show seriousness, rigor and perseverance, without dispersing. He will also have to show great determination, which will be necessary for him to face the numerous blockages and restrictions of his karma. It is by a sometimes hard work and in the long term that the debt will be rebalanced, but at the cost of big efforts on oneself.

If you have a major or minor challenge at value 1, 3 or 4, take it into account, as this will accentuate and complicate the debt.

The intensity of the energies in the inclusion grid :

In the grid of inclusion, it is necessary to check the intensity of the energies of 1, 2, 3 and 4, to know if the debt is really active, major or sometimes minor.

Generally, if the debt is active, the 1 and the 3 are in strong intensity in the inclusion, it will also be necessary to check if there is presence of 1 and 3 in the rest of the theme, then looked if the 2 and the 4 are missing or in weakness, in inclusion and in the theme. In some cases the 4 could also be in strong intensity, which would make the individual too stubborn and uncompromising, on the lookout for the slightest detail. This will give another color to the debt 13.

All this must be well analyzed, before drawing definitive conclusions.

Karmic debt 14/5: represents the domain of 5

14 = 1 + 4 = 5

Is also symbolized by the **"arcane temperance"** tarot

Karmic debt 14 means an abuse of personal freedom that may affect the addictions sector, such as exacerbated and disproportionate sexuality, alcohol and / or narcotics abuse, the individual may have been dependent on artificial paradises, be unfaithful and particularly unstable. These excesses of behavior harmed others, the individual having an attitude, again selfish and authoritarian, made of impulsiveness, but also of aggressiveness and imprudence. With a debt of this type, the pleasures of the senses were pushed to their paroxysm, sometimes putting the individual himself in danger, by dint of experiencing again and again all that could give him pleasure or change, the making it particularly unstable and irresponsible.

It is therefore in this incarnation necessary to temper these ardor, and his thirst for freedom and excessive discovery, a little more frame will not hurt, better structured this debt will be better apprehended, the experimentation to excess is never good, it will be necessary to show a fair measure in its acts.

If the debt is at the level of spiritual momentum :

this indicates sentimental, emotional problems and deep desires.

If the debt is at the expression level :

disappointments and problems in the material and professional field, but also in other areas.

If the debt is at the level of the life path :

there are risks of loss and failure in all areas of life.

In this incarnation, tests specific to this debt will be put on the path of the subject, or he will have to show adaptability and stability, moderation in his personal energies, in order to channel them well, the individual will have to be more structured, which will make it much more reliable for people and their families.

If you have a major or minor challenge worth 1, 4 or 5, take it into account, as this will accentuate and complicate the debt.

The intensity of the energies in the inclusion grid :

In the grid of inclusion, it is necessary to check the intensity of the energies of 1, 4 and 5, to know if the debt is really active, major or sometimes minor.

In general, if the debt is active, the 1 and the 5 are in strong intensity in the inclusion, it will also be necessary to check if there is presence of 1 and 5 in the rest of the theme, then looked if the 4 is missing or weak, in inclusion and in the theme. If the 4 is strong in the theme, it will channel 5 and disable the debt.

All this must be well analyzed, before drawing definitive conclusions.

Karmic debt 16/7: represents the domain of 7

16 = 1 + 6 = 7
Is also symbolized by the **"arcane house god"** tarot

This karmic debt indicates that one has ignored the feelings of his partner (s), or play with them, disappointments and upheavals, as well as emotional problems are to be feared in this incarnation. Be careful also about how you behave with your family and friends.

It is the Karma of the forbidden love stories, the karma of the marriage, the harm done to others, to the other, because of a totally irresponsible behavior, leading to very bad choices. The emotional structure has been strongly upset, undermining the sentimental balance, but also as is often the case, the other areas, by boomerang effect.

All this was brought about by a misunderstanding, a lack of objectivity of the emotional and amorous feeling, having probably caused a distorted vision in this field, but also by a behavior, still and always very selfish, and a temperament personality, the temperament of the individual having been very difficult and authoritarian, to note that the authoritarian tendency in the debt 16, is not systematic, which means that according to the intensity of the 1 in the inclusion, it is missing, weak or in excess, will still allow the debt to be active, unlike the other three debts, 13, 14 and 19 where the intensity of raising 1 is one of the main drivers.

There is a probability that the karmic debt could have been lived on the mental plane from the inside, through secret and unacknowledged thoughts. If it has been lived on the concrete level, it can also touch a sensitive and prohibited area of love, remain perhaps secret, or having been disclosed to the greatest number. If the excess of authority is proven, the individual was able to exercise it in the marriage, but also at the level of the family probably.

If the debt is at the level of spiritual impetus :

it indicates problems in the sentimental field and deep desires, quite serious.

If the debt is at the expression level :

disappointments and serious problems in the material field are also topical.

If the debt is at the level of the life path :

risks of losses of all kinds, goods, home, love, work are on the agenda, but do not panic, take a step back.

The karmic debt 16 can in some cases be particularly heavy consequences, leading to major upheavals in all areas of life.

In this incarnation, the individual will have to demonstrate a flawless reflection, do not hesitate to understand what is wrong, and open his mind through, if necessary a deep introspection. Affective relationships will certainly be difficult in this incarnation, made of conflicts, misunderstanding and rupture. Specific tests of this debt will be put on the path of the subject. The number 16 induces great upheavals, it cleanses and purifies what needs to be, to allow the soul to start on better foundations, just like the 13. It will not hesitate to review its old thought patterns for that.

If you have a major or minor challenge at value 1, 6 or 7, take it into account, as this will make the debt more accentuated and complicating.

The intensity of the energies in the inclusion grid :

In the grid of inclusion, it is necessary to check the intensity of the energies of 1, 6 and 7, to know if the debt is really active, major or sometimes minor.

Generally, if the debt is active, the 1 is in strong intensity in inclusion or weakness and the 6 and 7 in weakness or missing, it will also be necessary to check if there is presence of the 1 and the 6 and the 7 in the rest of the theme.

All this must be well analyzed, before drawing definitive conclusions.

The karmic debt 19/1 : represents the domain of 1

$19 = 10 = 1 + 0 = 1$
Is also symbolized by the **"arcane sun"** at tarot

Karmic debt 19 is in essence closely related to the abuse of authority, so it means an abuse of power in a previous life. It is a debt that has a wide scope, because it can operate in all areas of life and in all respects without any restrictions. Here the ego is really in the foreground, the motivations of the subject were totally dictated by the desire to exercise an important power and to have the ascendancy over others.

The 1 as you know it represents the individual, and the 9 represents the others, the community, a more or less large group of individuals, having had to undergo the authoritarianism of a single person, motivated by its own interests. Note in passing, that if the 1 is in weakness in the inclusion and in the theme, it is unlikely that the subject could submit a large group of individuals to his will alone.

If the debt is at the level of the spiritual impulse :

difficulties to fulfill these personal desires, to assert oneself, to have confidence in him.

If the debt is at the expression level :

disappointments and problems in life in general, material losses, delays, inducing frustrations and emotional and nervous tensions can occur.

If the debt is at the level of the life path :

proof of independence, material and emotional losses, oppositions to personal achievements, especially if you have a minor or major challenge 1.

In this incarnation, the subject will have to show more compassion towards others, of humility, he will have to position itself more as a guide, that executioner, he will have to face the tests head tall and to keep confidence in his potential director, the notion of power will have to be approached objectively in the service of others.

These are tests related to authority that will be put on the path of the subject, imposing in turn the need to be confronted with the power of others, or a hierarchy.

If you have a major or minor challenge at value 1 take it into account, as this will accentuate and complicate the debt.

The intensity of the energies in the inclusion grid :

In the grid of inclusion, it is necessary to check the intensity of the energies of 1, 2 and 9, to know if the debt is really active, major or sometimes minor.

Generally, if the debt is active, the 1 is in strong intensity in the inclusion and the low or missing 9, as well as the 2. It will also be necessary to check if there is presence of 1, 2 and 9 in the rest of the theme. In the case where the 9 would be in strong intensity, the debt would be of minor influence.

All this must be well analyzed, before drawing definitive conclusions.

Minor karmic debts

The minor karmic debts are five in number.

As its name indicates, their influences are much less important than the major debts, they are not always active, it is according to the general theme, like the major debts but in a smaller importance, but it is always judicious d take this into account.

The five minor debts: **11**, **12**, **15**, **18** and **26**

Minor karmic debt 11 :

Tarot 11 is represented by the **"arcane force"**.

The 11th is, as you know, a superior vibration, it is a master number, its energy is very specific and particularly powerful. Symbolically, it is a spiritual vibration of a very high level. But in the negative, it can wreak havoc.

With debt 11, we can find some aspects of the major debt 19, at the level of authority, the management of personal power and the ascendancy over others. It could be in some cases, in support of debt 19, following certain themes containing both debts 19 and 11. If the theme in question is strong in 1, 4 and 8, and low in 2, 6 and 9 it may be that we have to do in this extreme case, a dictator, or a guru, if the 11 is lived at its highest level, in its negative aspects. To a lesser extent, this will be a minor debt 11, with a much more attenuated scope.

If the theme is looked at in a negative way, double 1 will inevitably induce the authoritarian and egotistical aspects inherent in this vibration. As is often the case with karmic debts, the problems come from a non-objective view of reality, and from not grasping the real opportunities of evolution that presents itself to us.

This inevitably leads to delays and delays, which prevent the individual from being carried out properly.

In this incarnation, the subject will have to channel his personal energies and internal tensions, his anxiety, to avoid imposing his vision of things, and to use his personal power for more humanistic purposes.

If the 11 in minor debt is one or more key positions of the theme, and if it never vibrates in 2 positive, this can be problematic in all areas of life, conflicts will be numerous.

If you have a major or minor challenge at value 1 take it into account as this will accentuate the problems.

The intensity of the energies in the grid of inclusion :

In the grid of inclusion, it is necessary to check the intensity of the energies of 1 and 2 to know if the debt is really active.

Generally, if the debt is active, the 1 is in strong intensity in the inclusion and the 2 missing, it will also be necessary to check if there is presence of 1 and 2 in the rest of the theme, and check the others numbers as always, for the sake of clarity.

All this must be well analyzed, before drawing definitive conclusions.

The minor karmic debt 12 :

Tarot 12 is represented by the "**arcane hangman**".

Debt 12 represents a problem related to communication and listening, it indicates a self-centered and very selfish personality, having tended to disperse, and to make errors of way, by making decisions inappropriate. In this incarnation you could be misunderstood, people not listening to you. Back forced, because you certainly were not you too in a previous life, too concerned about yourself. The individual in a previous life had to express himself, within the different partnerships, by imposing himself and listening to himself speak, impacting the sensibility of others by superficial and selfish attitudes, probably devaluing, using lies and of gossip.

In this incarnation it is therefore necessary to be more attentive to others, but also to one's spouse, to be more aware of those around you, and to let those who wish to express themselves Everyone has the right to express themselves, without necessarily keeping the spotlight on the scene.

This minor debt can affect all areas of life.

If you have a major or minor challenge at values 1, 2 and 3 consider this, as this will accentuate the problems.

The intensity of the energies in the grid of inclusion :

In the grid of inclusion, it is necessary to check the intensity of the energies of the 1, 2 and 3 to know if the debt is really active.

Generally, if the debt is active, the 1 is in strong intensity in the inclusion and the 2 and the 3 missing or very weak, it will also be necessary to check if there is presence of 1, 2 and 3 in the rest of the theme.

All this must be well analyzed, before drawing definitive conclusions.

The minor karmic debt 15 :

Tarot 15 is represented by the **"arcane devil"**.

Karmic debt 15 is a debt of abuse of power and abuse of liberty within the family and relatives. We find the authoritarian and egocentric tendencies used to dominate his loved ones, while abusing a freedom of action that prejudices them.

The individual in an earlier incarnation, has been particularly attached to the pleasures of a sexual order, and that in excess. In some cases he was able to abuse the other, sometimes under duress. The subject's desires have become obsessive, falling into the consuming passion and collecting the partners. All this makes him consciously or not, the notion of responsibility in the family and probably in the professional field. The individual must certainly abuse his power of seduction, his magnetism and his charisma on a daily basis. There is with the debt 15, also the notion of lust, easy money, spent for the benefit of the personal pleasures, in the game also why not. This karmic debt is broader than we think, and its influence is on the notion of enslavement.

action that prejudices them.

The individual in an earlier incarnation, has been particularly attached to the pleasures of a sexual order, and that in excess. In some cases he has been able to abuse the other, sometimes In this incarnation, the subject will have to take his responsibilities and take care of his relatives, he will have to channel his impulses and his personal energies, in order to maintain the balance and the harmony to serve instead of enslaving, protecting instead of attacking.

If you have a major or minor challenge at values 1, 5 and 6, consider this as this will accentuate the problems.

The intensity of the energies in the grid of inclusion :

In the grid of inclusion, it is necessary to check the intensity of the energies of 1, 5 and 6 to know if the debt is really active.

Generally, if the debt is active, the 1 is in strong intensity in the inclusion as well as the 5 and the 6 missing or very weak, it will also be necessary to verify if there is presence of the 1, the 5 and the 6 in the rest of the theme.

All this must be well analyzed, before drawing definitive conclusions.

The minor karmic debt 18 :

In tarot the 18th is represented by the "**arcane moon**".

Debt 18 is the search for exaggerated power, to the detriment of others. The individual in a previous life to abuse his authority and personal power for purposes of personal ambition. Using all possible means available to it. His combative determination without flaws, allowed him to satisfy his desires in all areas, submitting to his will the community. Ignoring the emotions and feelings of others, without empathy the subject could use the weakest and most manipulable to achieve his ends.

In this incarnation, the subject will have to show more empathy, and consideration towards the others, he will have to use his personal power at the service of the community, not to serve his desires, but for the needs of the greatest number.

If you have a major or minor challenge at value 1 and 8 consider it, as this will accentuate the problems.

The intensity of the energies in the grid of inclusion :

In the grid of inclusion, it is necessary to check the intensity of the energies of 1, 8 and 9 to know if the debt is really active.

Generally, if the debt is active, the 1 and the 8 are in strong intensity and the 9 missing or very weak, it will also be necessary to check if there is presence of 1, 8 and 9 in the rest of the theme.

All this must be well analyzed, before drawing definitive conclusions.

The minor karmic debt 26 :

Debt 26 is a debt that weakens the will of the subject, makes it uncomfortable or not at all, without any ambition, having difficulties in realizing itself and approaching the notion of money as it should be. It is also likely that there are physical problems, this debt can be active in all areas of life.

The subject has been able in a previous life to feel devalued, or inferior, without doing what it takes to get out, unable to take things in hand and indulge in ease.

In this incarnation, the subject will have to be more combative, voluntary and determined, to face certain failures, in particular in his personal enterprises but also to face precariousness, material and financial losses. He will have to develop his will and self-confidence to make it happen.

If you have a major or minor challenge worth 2 6 and 8 take it into account, as this will accentuate the problems.

The intensity of the energies in the grid of inclusion :

In the grid of inclusion, it is necessary to check the intensity of the energies of 2, 6 and 8 to know if the debt is really active.

Generally, if the debt is active, the 2 is in strong intensity in the inclusion the 1 missing or very weak, the 8 probably weakens, but not always. It will also be necessary to check if 1, 2, 6 and 8 are present in the rest of the theme.

All this must be well analyzed, before drawing definitive conclusions.

In conclusion :

What must be kept of all this, the reality is simple in reality, the human being with the will, want to impose his ideas and ideals to the greatest number, to establish his domination in any form whatsoever. If the individual can not have the ascendancy over the greatest number, then he will exercise it over a small part, and even to the nearest ones. The human being has a lot of work to do before reaching the ultimate evolution, he still has a lot of things to learn in order to rise.

The successive incarnations of the soul serve this purpose.

As long as the lessons of life are not learned, the individual will not stop, trying to improve, at the cost of great effort.

Karmic accumulation

What is karmic accumulation? It is simply, when one finds several debts and karmas in a theme. One can, as is often the case with a heavy karmic liability, so it will be necessary to relate the different karmic debts (always with the grid of inclusion) to obtain valuable information.

For example, if in a theme you find a debt of abuse of liberty, and a debt of abuse of authority and of liberty, it will be obvious that the notion of personal freedom has been scorned at most. high level.

Another example, with a debt of abuse of authority and a debt linked to unfinished tasks, it is quite likely that the excess of authority may have been used in the area of the 4 in addition to the 1, but is the study of the complete theme that will confirm it.

There is also the possibility of having three or four karmic debts, in addition to the karmas of inclusion. But do not panic, there are always solutions, and do not focus all the time on it and stop yourself from living.

Karmic accumulation, of course, concerns karmic lessons as well as karmic debts.

Karmic accumulation at the level of lessons :

If you have, for example, 2 and 8 in karmic lesson in the inclusion, you have a karmic accumulation with value 10, because 2 + 8 = 10

If you have, for example, the 3 and the 7 in karmic lesson in the inclusion, you also have a karmic accumulation with value 10. Except that the origin will not be the same.

Last example, with three karmic lessons, 1, 6 and 8 you will have a karmic accumulation to swallow 15.

The interpretation table, will then give you additional interesting information to help you rebalance your cumulation of karma.

See the complete interpretation table at the end of the book for more information.

Karmic accumulation at the level of major debts :

I set up a new karmic accumulation method for major and minor debts.

There are 9 possible karmic accumulations at the level of major debts.

Table of karmic accumulation of major debts :

1	2	3	4	5	6	7	8	9
1	3	4	5	6	7	8	9	11

The first line represents the 9 possible karmic accumulations. The domain of 2 being absent.
The second line represents the final vibrations of karmic accumulations, after the addition of karmic debts.
We will see how it works, with the example below.
If you have four karmic debts, 13,14, 16 and 19, you add them up without reducing them.

13 + 14 + 16 + 19 = 62 = 8

All you have to do is interpret 8 on the table above and on the interpretation table of karmic accumulations of major debts.
If you have two karmic debts, 14 and 16, you add them up without reducing them.

14 + 16 = 30 = 3

All you need to do is interpret 3 on the table above and on the interpretation table of karmic accumulations of major debts.

Depending on the major debts that you will find in a numerology theme, simply add them up without reducing them, and refer to the table above, as well as to the interpretation table, at the end of the book. .

You will always get a sub-number, which you can also interpret, to qualify the final number if you wish.

The interpretation table, will give you additional interesting information to help you rebalance your cumulation of karma.
See the complete interpretation table at the end of the book for more information.

Karmic accumulation at the level of minor debts :

1	2	3	4	5	6	7
1	3	5	6	7	8	11

The first line represents the 7 possible minor karmic accumulations. The domains of 2, 4 and 9 being absent. The second line represents the final vibrations of karmic accumulations, after the addition of karmic debts.

* The operation is exactly the same as with the major debts.

Depending on the major debts that you will find in a numerology theme, simply add them up without reducing them, and refer to the table above, as well as to the interpretation table, at the end of the book. .
You will always get a sub-number, which you can also interpret, to qualify the final number if you wish.
The interpretation table, will then give you additional interesting information to help you rebalance your

cumulation of karma.
See the complete interpretation table at the end of the book for more information.

Part two

Karmic analysis from concrete examples

In this second part, we will study, analyze and put in situation the karmic debts, always in relation with the grid of inclusion, and the various key positions of a theme. We will study a very detailed profile for that.

Karmic letters :

Note: In the alphabet, each letter has a specific place,

Letter **M = 13**
Letter **N = 14**
Letter **P = 16**
Letter **S = 19**

These letters are not necessarily karmic, so do not systematically consider them, unless there are active karmic debts of the same values in a theme. If there are none, these letters must be interpreted normally.

It's the same for minor debts,

Letter **K = 11**
Letter **L = 12**
Letter **O = 15**
Letter **R = 18**
Letter **Z = 26**

Karmic birth days :

At the level of major karmic debts, birthdays corresponding to 13, 14, 16 and 19.

At the level of minor karmic debts, the corresponding birthdays are 11, 12, 15, 18 and 26.

All these elements must be related to the whole natal and annual theme, to define the influence of different karmic debts.

As you will see in the detailed study that follows, I will put all the elements in relation to each other, the karmic debts, the grid of inclusion and its karmic lessons, the excesses of the grid and the theme, the challenges.

Karma is not just about debts, lessons and challenges, but about the whole natal and annual theme.

Study :

Study of Marie Michelle Madeleine Debaurans, born 09/12/1956

Active number 1: which comes from 109 = **19** = 10 = 1
Number of heredity 5: which comes from 32 = 5
Number of Expression 6 (karmic): who comes from 141 = 6
Number of spiritual impulse 6 (Vowels, karmic): who comes from 69 = **15** = 6
Number of accomplishment 9 (consonants): who comes from 72 = 9
Life Path 6 (karmic): who comes from 33 and 24
Life Path Challenges: 6 (Karmic) in Major and Minor Challenge.

Marie, to a **13/4** value karmic accumulation, obtained by adding her two karmic lessons 6 and 7.

And a karmic accumulation at the level of the debts, with value 62/8, obtained by adding, the debt **13**, **14**, **16** and **19**.

The dominant numbers vibration theme:

It is important to have an overview of a theme, to highlight the most important vibrations of it, and to highlight the major trends of a personality, at the level of key positions.

The domains of 1, 3, 4, 5 and 9 in the inclusion, are in a dominant position.

The initials M with the three first names and the D of the name, give all, the value 4. What makes the number 4 particularly dominant in the theme, and even in excess. The number 9 is also present, in the inclusion, in the spiritual impulse and in the day of birth.

The number 6 is dominant, the way of life, the number of expression and the spiritual impulse.

The numbers 4, 6 and 9 largely define the personality of Mary. The 3 is found in a dominant position in the cycles of the life path, as well as 6 and will define certain types of events, related to these two numbers.

* Note in passing that the active number has a root 109 and 19 in reduction.

* Note also the three M's in the initials of the first names with a value of 13/4

Analysis of karmic debts in the identity :

M	A	R	I	E	Total
4	1	9	9	5	28/1
M 4 + R 9 = **13/4** to consonants					

In the first name Mary, we find the karmic debt 13 at the level of the consonants in terms of concrete achievements, the M marries worth 13/4 in this case, could be an indicator, it will be necessary to study the general theme to know if there is an active debt.

M	I	C	H	E	L	L	E	Total
4	9	3	8	5	3	3	5	40/4
I 9 + E 5 + E 5 = **19/1** to vowels									

This time we find the debt 19 at the level of the vowels, on the affective plane and the deep desires, but also on the level of the active number 1, having a root 109 and 19 in reduction.

M	A	D	E	L	E	I	N	E	Total
4	1	4	5	3	5	9	5	5	41/**14**/5
M 4 + D 4 + L 3 + N 5 = **16**/7 to consonants									
Debt 14 appears by totaling the letters									

As we can see, **Madeleine** has two karmic debts with a value of **16** and **14**. The debt 14 is in secondary reduction, is perhaps not active, or minor influence, but we will see that further. The debt 16, is at the level of vowels and deep desires, and the debt 14 in the totality of the letters of the first name.

The surname **DEBAURANT**, contains no karmic debt, nor the path of life. We will now look at the inclusion grid for Marie's complete identity.

Inclusion grid or intensity of Marie Debaurant :

1	2	3	4	5	6	7	8	9
4	2	5	5	9	0	0	1	5
					d			
					k	k		

The average equilibrium for this profile is 3.44, to obtain this average, it suffices to add all the letters of the identity and to divide by 9. The number of letters contained in the complete identity is 31.

Let's detail this grid before using it at the level of karmic debts. The small d represents the challenges, and the small k, the karmic lessons.

The box of 1 is well filled, it is a 1 hard, but structured by 4. The 1 to the asset makes it dominant, and gives it even more intensity in the theme.

The box of 2 is also occupied by a 2, it is however rather weak, because below the equilibrium average, and little or not represented in the theme.

The box of 3 is occupied by a 5, it is above the average of equilibrium, but little or not represented in the theme, except in the cycles of life, its intensity is slightly dominant, without more.

The box of 4 is also occupied by a 5, it is above the average of equilibrium, and particularly present in the

theme, especially at the level of the M of the three first names.
Its intensity is dominant, I would say even in excess.

The box of 5 is occupied by a 9, it is well above the equilibrium mean, it is also present in the theme, and appears three times in the inclusion, at box 3, 4 and 9. Its intensity in the theme is particularly important, especially in inclusion, it is most certainly the pivotal number of the theme, the energy on which our dear Marie relies first.

The box of 6 is occupied by a zero, so it is missing, but very present in the theme, has important positions, such as the number of expression, the spiritual impulse and the way of life. This is not a new lesson, but for me it is still karmic, because its important presence in the theme, shows that its potential has already been used in a previous life. It is also accompanied by a major and minor challenge 6, the whole makes it particularly badly considered in the theme, its influence is negative for the subject, which has not settled some negative aspects of the 6.

The box of 7 is occupied by a zero, the 7 is not at all represented in the theme or so little, so here is a real lesson to learn, the potential of 7 is lacking and has never been exploited in a previous life , which is a problem in terms of the debt 16, it seems obvious to me.

The box of 8 is occupied by the 1, the 8 as much in the theme as in the inclusion, at a very weak intensity.

The box of 9 is occupied by a 5, it is above the average equilibrium and its intensity is important especially as the number of Marie's achievement is also a 9.

We will now be able to define the intensity of the various karmic debts of Marie Debaurant.

The intensity of karmic debts :

The theme of Mary, contains the four major karmic debts best known in numerology, we will see if they are active and what are their intensities and their influences.

The debt 13, appears in the first name Marie to the consonants, and in the M of the three first names.
In the first part of the book it says, to check at the level of the intensity of the numbers 1, 2, 3 and 4 to know if the debt 13 is active.

For this, the 1 and the 3 must be strong, the 2 weak or missing, and the 4 is weak or missing, or in strong intensity.

If we check this at the level of the inclusion, we realize that it is indeed the case, the 1 and the 3 are in strong intensity, the 3 being also pushed by the 5 very strong in the inclusion. The 2 as we have seen is present but weak, and the 4 is in excess, the debt is active, and major influence, with a tendency to maniaquerie, stubbornness, excess of authority, and on the lookout for the slightest detail, because of the 4 in excess, and the 1 which is powerful. In the 1 of the inclusion, resides a 4, which confirms to us that the authority of the 1 is fed by the obstinacy and the intransigence of the 4, with the level of the debt 13, all this being finally managed in a scattered way , by the 3 strong. We can therefore conclude that Mary has not yet settled her debt, 13 or that she has great difficulty in doing so, for her soul has returned to this life with the same pitfalls.

Notons au passage, au actif, au-dessus du plan de réalisation concret, 13 contenu dans les trois éléments initiaux, qui doivent être pris en compte, comme un indicateur supplémentaire, 13 existe dans l'identité, dans le cas où il a été facilement annulé.

Debt 14, appears in the name Madeleine, consonants and vowels. In the first part of the book it says, check at the level of the intensity of the numbers 1, 4 and 5 to know if the debt 14 is active. For that, the 1 and the 5 must be in strong intensity, and the 4 in weak or missing.

As for the 1 and 5, it is the case they are both rather strong in intensity, but the 4 is too, which means that if the 4 is powerful, he was able to channel impulses of 5, and if we also take into account that the debt 14 is not in direct reduction, but secondary, we could say that it is not active in this case, but if we take into account the significant presence of 5 in the inclusion, and the 4 in the theme and inclusion, it still indicates some behavioral excesses so minimal.

Debt 16, appears in the name Madeleine at the level of consonants. In the first part of the book it says, check at the level of the intensity of the numbers 1, 6 and 7 to know if the debt 16 is active. For that the 1 must be in strong intensity or weakness, in both cases the debt may be active, but decrease if the 1 is weak, and the 6 and 7 must be either weak or missing.

We find that the 1 is high intensity in this case, and the 6 and 7 missing in the inclusion, which confirms us that the debt is actually active.

However, it is interesting to note that the 6 is very present in the theme contrary to the 7, and that it is also under the aegis of a major and minor challenge at value 6. The 6 being very negative in the theme, with the 1 in high intensity, the debt 16 is certainly at its maximum intensity.

Its influence is present in all areas of life, the negative 6 is an important indicator, since contained in the debt 16. I will go even further, taking into account that the 6 of spiritual impulse comes from a 69/15, one could see the influence at a low level of the minor debt 15, which is a debt of abuse of authority and freedom in the field of family and relatives, represented by 15 / 6 (see detailed meaning in the first part of the book). But if it is active, it will be weak. However the debt 15/6 touches the area of 6, which is karmic in the theme and present in the debt 16. I conclude from the view of the whole of the study of Mary, that this area of 6 is particularly touched by his karma.

Debt 19, appears in the name Michelle to vowels. In the first part of the book it says, to check at the level of the intensity of the numbers 1, 2 and 9 to know if the debt 19 is active. For that the 1 must be in strong intensity, and the

2, the 9 in weakness or missing. The 9 if it is high intensity as the 1 may indicate that the debt is minor or low.

In our case the 1 is actually in high intensity, the 2 in weakness and the 9 in high intensity too. There is no trace here of a major active debt, but there is a probability that it is a minor or weak influence, because again of the 5 particularly present in the inclusion, Indeed, the 5 is in the domain of the 9th and the 9th is in the domain of the 5, which would indicate, not an abuse of power, but rather an excess of selfishness in general in an earlier life, also confirmed by the 5 in the domain of the 3 at the level of inclusion. Let us note in passing that the 1, 3, 5, 8 and 9 carry the notion of selfishness and that they can accentuate this trait of character. Egoism always present in this life, if we look at the theme.

In conclusion marries four karmic debts in its theme, debt 13, 14, 16 and 19.

Debt 13 is active and with major influence, debt 14 can be considered as having very minor influence.
Debt 19 is also minor in influence or weak, emphasizing egoism.
Debt 16 is a major influence, especially since 6 is a karmic lesson in inclusion, but also as a major and minor challenge at a time, indicating a very important lack of responsibilities to work on in this life. this problem is recurrent, that is why debt 16 exists. In the light of the theme, the subject certainly showed a selfishness without half-measure, which he has not yet solved.

The karmic 7 in inclusion confirms this, as well as the presence of the major debt 16. The negative 7 induces a lack of understanding and distorts the feeling of love, it is undisciplined, the negative 6 irresponsibility and egoism, the jealousy. The soul of Mary must do an important job in order to evolve, and for me the 6 is one of the pivots of this karmic instability, accompanied by a very dominant 5, certain impulses must be difficult to control, but still channel in part by a 4 very present.

The major negative aspects that emerge from this theme are related to a great deal of egoism, excessive authority, intransigence, and a blatant lack of open-mindedness on the part of Mary in a previous life, which did not obviously not taking into consideration the desires of others, perhaps also out of jealousy. In this life, Mary's soul came back with the same defects, to allow her to rebalance her karma, by imposing situations that put her in front of her responsibilities.

Marie, to a karmic accumulation of value 13, obtained by adding her two karmic lessons 6 and 7.

This karmic accumulation proposes to him, to adapt to the radical changes of its existence, with its capacity to rebound, that is how it will be able to use the potential of the 6 and the 7 karmic. She will also have to use her will and determination without abusing it, as well as her ability to communicate.

His second karmic accumulation, resulting from the addition of his four debts, is worth 8. It is proposed to him to have a good management of his personal power, associated with a measured combativity which will help him in his approach of karmic rebalancing if his qualities fail him, it will be necessary to develop them, but without ever falling into the excesses of 8.

Karma in the cycles of life and annual :

Marie Life Path Cycle Chart :

3	9	3	
21/3	21/3	42/6	24/6

The first line represents the three life cycles of the life path, worth 3, 9 and 3.
The second line represents the four climaxes of the way of life of Mary, swallower 3, 3, 6 and 6.

We note on the one hand the important presence of the number 3, which is also dominant in the inclusion. In the first part of life, we observe the superposition of the 3, between the first and second realization cycle and the first atmosphere cycle. This is the indicator of an exacerbated personal expression, a relationship rich in communication, an extroversion, but especially a scattering of personal energies, especially in the youth. The dominant 4 has been able to minimize the effects by structuring it. There is also a significant creative potential.

This 3, confirms me that the debt 13 is still active, or at least the summer in the first part of his life.

The last two cycles of realization, indicates well the presence of the 6 karmic, accompanied by the sub-numbers 42 and 24, with yin dominant energy, these are two important periods and of a particularly long duration, or our dear Marie, if it has not rebalanced his karma, will have to face his responsibilities in general and also to a certain fragility on the family and emotional level. On the last 24/6 value cycle, there could be betrayals and helpers from one or more women at the same time.

Since this 6 is present in the debt 16, there is therefore an obvious karmic relationship.

Table of the first and third annual cycle of realization for the personal year 6 :

We will now see Mary's annual cycles, if we see her karma clearly.

I will take the year 2019 and 2020 as an example, in 2019 our subject will be in personal year 6 and in 2020 in a personal year 7 coming from a 16. We can already see, that the personal years 6 and 7 will be two difficult years for our subject, and this at each passage of the nine-year cycle, as long as he has not rebalanced his karmas.

If we go up the full graph of Marie's personal year 6, which I leave you the leisure to realize in its entirety if you wish, to check and train, we can see (see the table below) that the first annual cycle of realization (which starts from January to March 2019), is worth 6 over a year 6, and that it will have as influence, the expression, the spiritual impulse, the way of life, the challenge and the karma worth 6 of Mary. It will be a particularly busy cycle in terms of concrete achievements, so there is a significant peak during this period that will require making the right choices, and certainly sacrifices in the area of 6. If we look at the third cycle annual realization, we have again the same value cycle 6 that comes back, it tells us two important karmic peaks in this personal year 6.

AP 6 k											
climaxes	3				5				8		
production	6 k			9			6 k			9	
personal months	7k	8	9	1	11	3	4	5	6k	7k	8	9

The k indicates where are the karmic vibrations of the personal year, the two cycles of realization, and the personal months, the 7 do not forget being also karmic, but in new lesson, which is in my opinion also one of the reasons for the presence of debt 16/7.

If we look more closely at the annual climaxes 3 and 5, again looking at the inclusion grid, as we already know, these two areas are very intense, it is very likely that our Marie, has serious difficulties to rebalance his personal energies and his karma.

This is quite normal, as you know, we do not solve behavioral problems and some traits of our character overnight. Must we want it?

Table of the first annual cycle and second climax for the personal year 7/16 :

	AP **7/16** debt karmic									
climaxes	**3**				**6k**			**9**		
production	**7k**				**1**			**8**	**11**	
Personal months	8	9	1	11	3	4	5	**6k**	**7k**	8	9	1

The k indicates the karmic vibrations of the year, the first cycle of realization is under the aegis of karmic 7, and the second climax is marked by karmic 6, as well as two of the personal months of the year.

What is important to remember is that the personal year 7 is a year that highlights the karmic debt 16 with major influence, Mary, as we have already seen elsewhere. What does that mean? Simply that it will be an important year at this level, that vibratory energies present that year, gives the opportunity to our study subject to try to rebalance this debt, because it will be put in front of its responsibilities, and will have according to the people, situations and opportunities present at that time. The period is likely to be complicated for her, especially since the most favorable or probable moment for this will be in the first realization cycle 7, starting from January to February 2020, as can be seen in the graph below. above. Probably even during personal month 9, because the 9 is a significant number in the theme of Mary, as well as in her inclusion, Mary to a number of achievements worth 9, found in a personal month 9, which is just in the realization cycle 7. The result is that the events will happen on the concrete plan, because as we know, as much for the number and the cycle of realization, it is the real actions of an individual who come true. The 9 symbolizes the emotions, the end or the conclusion of certain things, if we add it to the realization cycle 7, we get again the 16. That's how we can target in an annual theme, important events karmic or not, in all areas of life, but this is not the purpose of this book, which is centered on karmic numerology.

The study of our dear Marie, is now over, we will see now to deepen a little more, the few additional information necessary, which will allow you to go even further.

Other examples :

Example of a person born on 25/01/1941:

This is an existing profile, but will remain anonymous, with the agreement of the person in question.

Way of life: 23/**5**
Number of expression: **5**
Major challenge: **5**
Physical expression plan of letters: **5**
Inclusion grid, number intensity: 1, 5 and 9

The 1 and the 5 are in strong intensity, the 4 is present, but much weaker in the theme, the 9 to a 5 in its box.

Karmic debt : **14/5**

This karmic debt of abuse of personal liberty, appears three times, in two of the three first names, once in secondary reduction and twice in direct reduction.

The date of birth also contains the numbers 1, 4 and 5, always consider the numbers of the date of birth in a study.

This example is self-explanatory, the 14/5 debt is active, and at its major intensity level. Debt that has not been settled yet, and will follow the soul in her next life, if she decides to return.

If you find karmic debts in direct reduction, such as with the name Marc.

I add the letters M, R and C of marc, I get the number 16 to the consonants, so I have a karmic debt 16/7 in direct reduction.
If by adding a complete identity, which is called expression number, I get a 97, when I reduce it, it will give me, 97 = 9 + 7 = 16 = 1 + 6 = 7. This will be a number of expression 7, which comes from a 97/16, in this case I have a karmic debt in second reduction, which can tell me, what is not active or minor influence, unless I find it elsewhere in the subject of the person studied, because in some themes may appear several times the same karmic debt.

A debt in direct reduction is generally the indicator, that the karmic debt in question is active, and major.

Use the methods of the book to know it, as I did with the profile of Mary.
For a date of birth, it's the same thing.
For example, with the date of 02/01/2008, I get in direct reduction the number 13.
2 + 1 + 2 + 8 = 13 = 1 + 3 = 4, so I have a life path 4 from a 13. I therefore have a 13/4 karmic debt directly in the life path.
Whether in direct or secondary reduction, one can find karmic debts, in the whole of the complete identity and the way of life, in the consonants, the vowels, the number of expression, the active number, of heredity, the way of life, the cycles, the number of life, the day of birth, a little everywhere in fact.

Conclusion :

You now have all the tools, to determine the various karmic influences, to explore and go even further in this area. Always take a step back, and stay objective, everything is not karma or karmic.

Influences can be felt on all levels, according to each individual and each destiny, it will be up to you to determine how to approach your own karma and how to progress on your initiatory path.

www.numerologueconseils.com

Tables of interpretations

Karmic accumulation of lessons

If you have karmic accumulation 3:

It is through expression, communication and creativity that you will be able to develop and use your potential. Be careful not to scatter or fall into exuberance beyond measure.

If you have karmic accumulation 4:

It is through rigor, perseverance and will, that you will be able to develop and use your potential.
Be careful not to be too stubborn and closed.

If you have karmic accumulation 5:

It is through adaptability and acceptance of change that you will be able to develop and use your potential. Be careful not to fall into the excesses of all kinds, to be too impulsive.

If you have karmic accumulation 6:

It is through the notion of responsibility, balance and harmony, that you will be able to develop and use your potential. Be careful of the choice you make, and not to fall into excessive jealousy.

If you have karmic accumulation 7:

It is through reflection, introspection and analysis that you will be able to develop and use your potential. Think about opening your mind, you are not alone in the world.

If you have karmic accumulation 8:

It is through the management of your personal power, fighting spirit and willingness that you will be able to develop and use your potential. Be careful not to abuse this personal power, the backlash is never far away.

If you have karmic accumulation 9:

It is through humanism, the realization of your ideals and the management of your emotions, that you will be able to develop and use your potential. Be careful to manage your emotions well, and stay on your feet.

If you have karmic accumulation 10:

It is through adapting to change, your will and your determination that you will be able to develop and use your potential. Pay attention to a certain instability, and a fluctuation of the energies during the cycles.

If you have karmic accumulation 11:

It is through the management of your intuition, and the control of your energies, that you will be able to develop and use your potential. Your strength is an asset, but make sure to channel your energies and especially your nervous and emotional tensions.

If you have karmic accumulation 12:

It is through trials, sacrifice and communication that you will be able to develop and use your potential. Take the necessary distance, and act in calm and reflection, use your creative qualities.

If you have karmic accumulation 13:

It is by adapting to radical changes and your ability to bounce back that you will be able to develop and use your potential. Use your will and your creativity, your mind, without being too impulsive and scattered.

If you have karmic accumulation 14:

It is by channeling your excesses and the search for balance, that you will be able to develop and use your potential. Open your mind and use your will and determination, adapting yourself.

If you have karmic accumulation 15:

It is by channeling your excesses, your impulses and your passions, that you will be able to develop and use your potential. Pay attention to your impulsiveness, channel your personal energies, to maintain balance and harmony.

If you have karmic accumulation 16:

It is through many upheavals and many choices, that you will be able to develop and use your potential. Pay attention to your behavior, and not be too demanding with yourself, as well as with others, channel your mind.

If you have karmic accumulation 17:

It is through the use of your mental power and your will, and the aids that will be granted to you, that you will be able to develop and use your potential. Feel free to use your independence and your individuality, putting it at the service of a moderate power.

If you have karmic accumulation 18:

It is by your combative will and avoiding the pitfalls of destiny, that you will be able to develop and use your potential. Be careful not to abuse your personal power by putting it at the service of your ambitions, and this to the detriment of others.

If you have karmic accumulation 19:

It is through the use of your personal power in the service of the greatest number, that you will be able to develop and use your potential. It is by moderating your energies that you will achieve success and recognition.

If you have karmic accumulation 20:

It is through the use of your powerful intuition and sensitivity that you will be able to develop and use your potential. Pay attention to the fragility of this energy and your great sensitivity, your receptivity could be a precious help.

If you have karmic accumulation 21:

It is through expression, communication, creativity, and opportunities for success that you will be able to develop and use your potential. Be careful not to disperse and especially not to disperse your potential director.

If you have karmic accumulation 22:

It is by your great capacity of realization and your combative will, that you will be able to develop and use your potential. Pay attention to your stubbornness, which could slow you down in your large-scale achievements.

If you have karmic accumulation 23:

It is through expression, constant progression, and support, that you will be able to develop and use your potential. Be careful to channel your energies, and not be too unstable, which will allow you to evolve favorably.

If you have karmic accumulation 24:

It is through your sense of responsibility, your capacity for understanding and agreements and the management of your yin energies, that you will be able to develop and use your potential. Pay attention to your emotional fragility, be careful not to be overwhelmed by your emotions and sensitivity.

If you have karmic accumulation 25:

It is by managing the balance of your personal energies that you will be able to develop and use your potential. use your mind and your ambivalence to realize yourself.

If you have karmic accumulation 26:

It is through the management of your yin energies, your intuition and your will, that you will be able to develop and use your potential. Channel well your energies yin, so that it is not a dam to your concrete achievements.

If you have karmic accumulation 27:

It is through the management of your mind and your ability to step back, that you will be able to develop and use your potential. Stay alert to the management of your emotions, as they may take precedence over you.

If you have karmic accumulation 28:

It is through your ability to maintain balance and balance, that you will be able to develop and use your potential. Stay vigilant because there is some instability, it will be necessary to reconcile, but also sometimes to fight to advance.

If you have karmic accumulation 29:

It is through your creative qualities, and your great intuition, that you will be able to develop and use your potential. Channel your emotions and inner tensions well, what you will make use of your great spiritual strength.

If you have karmic accumulation 30:

It is through expression, communication and creativity at the highest level that you will be able to develop and use your potential. Channel well your energies and your tendency to express yourself excessively, in order to avoid scattering all your potential.

Karmic accumulation of major and minor debts

Karmic accumulation 1 : will, determination and self-confidence, you will help in the process of karmic rebalancing, if it is quality you lack, it will develop, but without ever falling into the excesses of 1.

Karmic accumulation 3 : communication, creativity and vivacity of spirit, you will help in the process of karmic rebalancing, if it is quality you lack, it will develop, but without ever falling into the excesses of the 3.

Karmic accumulation 4 : methodology, rigor and will, you will help in the approach of karmic rebalancing, if it is quality you lack, it will be necessary to develop them, but without ever falling into the excesses of the 4.

Karmic accumulation 5 : adaptability, open-mindedness and good management of your freedom of action, you will help in the process of karmic rebalancing, if it is quality you lack, it will develop, but without ever falling into the excesses of 5.

Karmic accumulation 6 : the sense of responsibility, the maintenance of the balance and the harmony in general, will help you in the approach of karmic rebalancing, if it is quality you lack, it will be necessary to develop them, but without never fall into the excesses of 6.

Karmic accumulation 7 : the reflection, the sense of the analysis and the capacity to take a step back will help you in the process of karmic rebalancing, if it is quality you lack, it will be necessary to develop them, but without ever falling into the excesses of 7.

Karmic accumulation 8 : a good management of your personal power, associated with a measured combativity will help you in the process of karmic rebalancing, if it is quality you lack, it will develop, but without ever falling into the excesses of 8.

Karmic accumulation 9 : the comprehension on a universal scale will help you in the process of karmic rebalancing, if it is quality you lack, it will be necessary to develop them, but without ever falling in the excesses of 9.

Karmic accumulation 11 : the use of your intuition, and your inner strength will help you in the process of karmic rebalancing, if it is quality you lack, it will develop, but without ever falling into the excesses of the 11

Karmic Lessons Interpretation or missing numbers of the inclusion

Take into account that even if there are no numbers in some cells of the inclusion, they can appear in the rest of the theme, it makes a real difference, because all the potentialities of a number missing in the inclusion will not necessarily be absent from the personality. It will then be necessary to qualify according to the different information obtained from the inclusion and the general theme. If there is no missing or karmic number in inclusion, it does not mean that there is no work to do on oneself.

The karmic 1 or when there are no letters of value 1 in your name and first name : in a previous life, we lacked self-confidence, we have not been able to assert ourselves and we have been dependent on others, may also indicate a problem with the father or absence of the father!

Life will take care of placing before us the trials necessary to make us evolve, make decisions, assert ourselves, show courage and respect ...

The 1 in excess : authoritarianism, will of domination, aggressive tendency, blockage of evolution.

The karmic 2 or when there are no letters of value 2 in your name and surname : In a previous life, you did not collaborate with others, you were insensitive to the feelings of others, in this life you should collaborate, cooperate and associate professionally and or personally without being dependent or submissive.

The 2 in excess: shyness, extreme emotivity, submission, lack of will, fear of others, assisted.

Karmic 3 or when there are no letters of value 3 in your name and surname : it symbolizes creativity and expression, in a previous life you could not or could express yourself,

You must have obeyed and submitted. In this life you will have the opportunity on many occasions to express yourself in public to develop your communication and your expression in all its forms and on all occasions ...

The 3 in excess: dispersion of energies without results, superficiality, great exuberance, hypocrisy jealousy.

Karmic 4 or when there are no letters of value 4 in your name and first name : In a previous life you have neglected the work and let others do for you, in this life you will have to learn how to build on solid foundations in stability and duration**.**

The 4 in excess : narrow-mindedness that limits progress and personal evolution, dogmatism, intransigence and strong obstinacy.

Karmic 5 or when there are no 5 value letters in your name and first name : the 5 in missing number is rather rare, but it happens to meet in a theme, in your previous life you have certainly shown of jealousy in relation to the freedom of others, in this life you will have to accept and adapt to changes that may be frequent, move and maybe even travel, be adaptable and avoid resistance to change.

The 5 in excess : scattering of personal energies, instability, excess of all nature according to the rest of the theme, unbridled sexuality, impulsiveness.

Karmic 6 or when there are no letters of value 6 in your name and first name : the 6 is mostly related to the karma of marriage, we had to miss these responsibilities in a previous life, we neglected the family, his spouse, the home, unable to assume these responsibilities towards the members of his family ...

The 6 in excess : excess of responsibility, lack of understanding of others, obstinacy, lack of open-mindedness, conservativer.

Karmic 7 or when there are no letters of value 7 in your first and last name : 7 is the number of faith and belief, whatever the area concerned, this karma is related to people who have not not enough open-minded, too closed, who only believed what they saw or touched, in this life you should be more open-minded and develop your inner faith, open yourself to other.

The 7 in excess : refocus on itself, mental too active, dogmatism, fanaticism, excessive introversion, ego very developed, hypersensitivity.

Karmic 8 or when there are no 8 letters of value in your first and last name : the 8 is related to the abuse of power and the law, as we know 8 is associated with the physical and physical aspects of life, in this life money and material success will not be obtained easily, the material and financial balance will be necessary, it will be necessary to show a fair measure in these acts and actions, in his personal judgment and towards others !

The 8 in excess : hyper materialism, no emotion or interest for others, thirst for power, uncompromising, obstinate, domineering and aggressive.

Karmic 9 or when there are no letters of value 9 in your first and last name : the 9 is very rarely missing as the 5, it indicates that one has lived withdrawn from the world, avoiding contact with others and not interested in human problems, in this life you will be faced with situations where you have to open up a little more to others, avoid selfishness and excess, show compassion and dedication without sacrificing yourself.

The 9 in excess : strong emotivity that impacts judgment, lack of objectivity, involving the individual in complicated situations, self-sacrifice, self-protection.

How to rebalance your karmic lessons :

The 1: To rebalance, You need to develop and understand the qualities of leadership you need, your courage and self-confidence without relying on the help of others, learn to assert yourself without imposing yourself, solve certain problems related to the male principle, men or the father if necessary.

The 2 : To rebalance, you will have to learn to associate and collaborate with others, learn understanding, be patient and diplomatic, accept others as they are without necessarily being subjected to them, without submitting to or being dependent on them, regulating problems related to the female principle, women or mother if necessary.

The 3 : To rebalance, you have to learn to express yourself without vanity or pride, develop communication and contact with others, develop your sociability in order to adapt, to overcome the blockages that prevent you from creating or expressing yourself as you would like .

The 4 : To rebalance, one must learn to build on solid foundations by stability and organization by showing patience and perseverance, without being too stubborn or passive. Sometimes you have to go beyond some of the obsolete thought patterns that prevent you from evolving, you also have to open your mind a little more.

The 5 : To rebalance, one must learn how to manage one's freedom, move and travel if necessary by living varied experiences, develop one's ability to adapt, and avoid excesses of all kinds, not to resist changes..

The 6 : To rebalance, we must develop the sense of family and professional responsibilities and understanding in the couple so that the union is harmonious. Do not be too demanding and make the decisions.

The 7 : In order to rebalance, one must develop one's inner faith by becoming more open-minded, detach oneself from the material aspect without concealing it, avoid fanaticism or isolate oneself in one's ivory tower, convinced of its superiority.

The 8 : To rebalance, you have to find the material balance, neither too much nor too little, the money and the professional success will not be obtained easily, a behavior, objective, fair and measured is advised, because the backlash is not never far away.

The 9 : To rebalance, one must develop compassion, be interested in human problems and others, avoid egoism, be more open, total isolation is not good, a minimum of empathy has never killed anyone.

Interpretation of Life Path Challenges

Challenge 1 : it is the challenge of opposition to personal achievements, the progression and the efforts are sometimes slowed down, difficulties to be imposed which generates aggressiveness, it is necessary to assert oneself and to have confidence in oneself, it can sometimes be necessary to individualize.

Challenge 2 : Challenge of submission, lack of confidence and assertiveness, high sensitivity, fragility and emotivity, avoid aggression, collaborate without submitting or being dependent.

Challenge 3 : challenge of communication, dispersion or superficiality, difficulties to express oneself, lack of openness according to the other parameters of the theme of the individual, reserved, timid ... critical with others, not to confine oneself ...

Challenge 4 : material and work-related deadlock, lack of open-mindedness, lack of structure and stability, tendency to let go, disorder ... must learn to structure.

Challenge 5 : challenge of personal freedom instability, impulsiveness, excess impatience for the pleasures of existence of all kinds, lack of structure. Learn how to structure, stabilize.

Challenge 6 : challenge of complacency, demanding, very attached to responsibilities, possessive, stifling, perfectionist, tyrannical, excess of tolerance, the individual carries the family burdens. Or conversely he is totally irresponsible and intolerant.

Challenge 7 : it is the challenge of isolation, reserved, introverted, pessimistic, anxious, critical and bad faith, perfectionist, difficulties in expressing these emotions, difficulty in realizing oneself, doubt and indecision, a mixture of pride and apparent humility. We must open ourselves to others.

Challenge 8 : challenge of materiality, opposition and obstacles, hard and rigid attitude, risks of errors in the career, thirst to provide, it is necessary to develop the human and spiritual dimension.

Symbolism and the foundation of numbers

This table can be used for the interpretation of many key and secondary numbers, for the rest you have available other interpretation tables that follow this one, as for example for the life path, the number of expression...

This table of general interpretation will allow you to understand on the one hand the fundamental meaning of the numbers, but also to use it for the interpretation of the various studies of the book, in addition to other tables of complementary interpretations. You can use it for all key positions in addition to information, as well as for sub-numbers too ...

The 1: Personal advancement by individual action, the creator

Dominant yang energy
Fire element
Odd number
Vibratory energy of dynamic and fast type
The father, the spouse, the man, the men in general, the leader, the one who directs and makes the decisions
Symbolizes the sky, the creator, the sun

At the level of character and personality:

Command, leadership, authority, Ego, individual action, individuality, self-realization, ambition, willpower, self-confidence, self-reliance, creativity, intelligence, isolation, selfishness, lies, impulsiveness, dynamism, daring, independence.

In terms of time and probable events:

The beginning, the departure, the new projects, the meetings, the hierarchy, start or new start.
The importance of the man or a man during the targeted period. Period or personal initiative is paramount. Will and determination are advised, while remaining measured in his actions.

The initiatory journey of the 1 : the learning of this lesson passes mainly by the individual himself, with sometimes the need to have to truly individualize in order to stand out substantially from others, and this in a positive approach. On the other hand this vibratory energy brings a certain creative dynamic potential, which you will have to use wisely. In order to be successful with this vibration, you will have to show determination, determination and confidence in yourself and in your own self-realization abilities. It's an important creative potential that has been put at your disposal, so that you can use it in the best way possible, without abusing your authority, or submitting and letting yourself be directed.

The 2 : Collaboration, union, intuition, sensitivity

Yin dominant energy
Water element
Odd number
Vibratory energy of slow and passive type
The mother, the wife, the wife, the women in general, the one who reconciles
Symbolizes the earth, the duality, the moon

Character and personality :

Collaboration, submission, cooperation and union, dependence, sensitivity, duality, listening ... submission, intuition, diplomacy, passivity, hypersensitivity, emotions, understanding , help, depression, sweetness, indecision.

In terms of time and probable events :

Probable contracts or association, union. Listen to your intuition and try to develop it.
The others are important, the receptivity and sensitivity can be exacerbated. There is less dynamism, not to let go,

less likely tone. Importance of one or more women during this period.

The initiatory journey of the 2 : Learning this lesson involves using your intuition and inner sensitivity. This vibratory energy gives you the necessary listening skills to be in harmony with others. As well as the ability to cooperate, to be able to help and understand, without allowing you to walk on it. Affirm what you are, to make you respect, and avoid letting yourself go.

The 3 : Communication, self-expression, creativity

Energy yang and yin, the yang remains dominant
Fire and air element
Odd number
Vibratory energy of dynamic and open type
The son, the child, the siblings, the one who expresses
Symbolizes the trinity, the spirit

Character and personality :

Sociability and communication, the ability to express oneself, contact, extroversion, creativity, enthusiasm, sometimes the dispersion of energies, intelligence, writings, hypocrisy, lies, superficiality, egoism, impulsiveness, aggression, appearances.

In terms of time and probable events :

Period when contacts are important, commercial transactions may be timely. The artistic field and writings are privileged, studies. Communication in all its forms is the center of the period concerned. Meetings are very likely, and many links can be created. Siblings and children can gain importance during this period.

The initiatory journey of the 3 : Learning this lesson involves personal expression, the expression of what you are fundamentally. The main focus is communication and its various ways of expressing it. This should be done in contact with others, while channeling your personal energies which depending on the case, can sometimes lead to a dispersion of these same energies. This vibration brings a very important creative potential, that you will have to use according to what you are and whatever your field of predilection.

The 4 : Work, the home, the structure of life, the bases

Yin dominant energy
Earth element
Even number
Vibratory energy of slow and static type
The focus, the roots, the solid structure, the one that builds in time
Symbolizes quaternary, stability, perseverance, frames.

Character and personality :

Ability to act concretely with order and method, sense of organization, sense of duty, rigor, rigidity and closure of mind, structure, will, stubbornness, patience and perseverance. Stubbornness, impulsiveness, aggressiveness, loyalty, reliability.

In terms of time and probable events :

Home and work are at the center of the period as are the administrations. Periods of blocking and slowing down are possible. The period is always conducive to building concrete things for the future. We must consolidate and stabilize the general structure of life, as well as readjust the old patterns of thought. The roots are important, as well as the family legacy, whether on a concrete and material level or on a mental and spiritual level.

The initiatory journey of the 4 : Learning this lesson involves respecting the frames and certain rules of life to understand. All this will have to be done with patience and perseverance. The structure of life, physical and mental, as well as the different hierarchical structures of our society, will have to be approached in an organized way, while maintaining a certain stability in time.

The 5 : Personal freedom and free will

Energy yang
Fire and air element
Odd number
Vibratory energy of dynamic type, fast and open
Movement and change, adaptability and discovery, whoever is experimenting
Symbolizes the man, the sexuality
The number 5 is at the crossroads, it is a hinge or central energy.

Character and personality :

Mobility and freedom, the ability to change and move, movement, change and dynamism, adventure, adaptability, instability, excesses, impulsiveness, sociability, sneaky spirit, piquancy in the words, exacerbated sensuality, the attraction for artificial paradises. Curiosity, experimentation, independence.

In terms of time and probable events :

It is often a period of change, movement and expansion, encounter and discovery. The period can be progressive. However, it is necessary to avoid any excess of behavior whatever the field, inducing instability. This is a time when you could have money coming in, as well as outings.

The initiatory journey of the 5 : The learning of this lesson requires good management of personal freedom, while adopting the most adaptable behavior possible. There is with this vibration, a notion of free will, perhaps more important than with other vibrations. Hence the importance of avoiding any excess of behavior that will lead to the failure and abuse of one's own freedom, but also to that of others.

The 6 : Harmony, love, choice and responsibility

Energy yin
Earth element
Even number
Vibrational energy of mixed type

Family, love and harmony, responsibilities
Symbolizes the woman, the sexuality

Character and personality :

Harmony and balance, gentleness, ability of conciliation and understanding, stability, sense of responsibility, doubts, indecision, choice, jealousy, requirement, love, feelings, The artist, the carer, jealousy and possessiveness, hyperemotivity.

In terms of time and probable events :

Family and home, sometimes a marriage, real estate transactions. The field of health can be topical. Love could knock on your door. But responsibilities and obligations are often at the center of this period.

Le cheminement initiatique du 6 : Learning this lesson involves the notion of harmony, choice and responsibility in all areas. Bad choices will inevitably lead to imbalance, undermining the overall harmony.

The 7 : The development of faith and the inner life, reflection

Energy yang
Water element
Odd number
Vibratory energy of slow and relatively quiet type
The solitary, the mystic, the technician, the one who creates by intellectual and spiritual force
Symbolizes Spirituality, the intellect, the divine

Character and personality :

The inner life, the capacity for analysis, reflection and diagnosis, independence, creativity, research, introspection, inner faith, rigidity, intransigence, fanaticism, isolation, requirement, spirituality, innovation, unpredictability, ability to step back, wisdom and inner discipline.

In terms of time and probable events :

Period of reflection, calm depending on the case, taking a step back. Opportunities may arise, the unexpected is also part of it. A tendency to introspection and ruminate, a balance can be done. Probable inner changes. Drop in tone possible. Favorable to research, studies, and writings.

The initiatory journey of the 7 : The learning of this lesson, through the development of his inner life which must be in adequacy with the external life, is a path of deep reflection and self-seeking necessary to evolve favorably. Time is the key.

The 8 : The power of realization

Energy yin and yang
Earth element
Even number
Vibratory energy of dynamic and combative type
Power and combativeness, material realization, the one who uses his power of realization

Symbolizes transformation, karma, the law of balance in all things, justice, death

Character and personality :

The ability to take on the physical plane, search for power and success, courage, will, energy, entrepreneurial desire, authority, ambition, business acumen and gains financial, combativeness, intransigence, law, the warrior.

In terms of time and probable events :

Combative period, or it is necessary to show will. It's an opportunity to use your personal power wisely. The law, the justice can be of the part, the financial structures, bank etc ... the business, the money and the financial aspect are of the part. There is also a notion of transformation and karma sometimes at work. It will be necessary to remain measured and fair in its actions, and to maintain an often precarious balance.

The initiatory journey of the 8 : Learning this lesson involves the notion of personal power and its proper use. This will maintain balance in everything, and stay measured in his actions and thoughts.
It is a karmic, transformational energy that is at work.

The 9 : Humanism, emotion

Energy yang and yin
Fire element
Odd number
Vibratory energy of dynamic and open type
Emotivity, intuition, psyche, others, the universal, the culmination, the one that opens to universal energies
Symbolizes spirituality, open-mindedness on a universal scale

Character and personality :

Altruism, the ability to take an interest in others, dreams and illusions, idealism, vocation, intuition, compassion, human sensitivity, emotions, dedication, self-sacrifice, losses, humanism, selfishness, jealousy, psyche, spirituality, jealousy, moodiness.

In terms of time and probable events :

Period of completion and conclusion, of losses too, it is often necessary to make a balance of the past. Emotions are exacerbated, sacrifice is sometimes necessary. We must open ourselves to the world, business related to a certain audience are involved, we must deal with others, the artistic and humanitarian fields are present and favored, egoism is to be avoided.

The initiatory journey of the 9 : The learning of this lesson, through the relationship to others, and how to behave in contact with external energies. This number is the culmination of the individual initiatory journey, the conclusion of a long spiritual walk. It is the quest for oneself within the universal cosmic principle. Humanism is the key.

11th and 22nd are specific vibrations called master numbers.

Consisting of twice the 1, it can be reduced to the number 2. In the case where the potential of 11 is not fully exploited, it will vibrate in 2. The 11 induces fundamentally strength, control and inspiration, but also nervous tension important. It is a receptive dual number and having a certain sensitivity, the 11 as the 22 can indicate by their presence that an evolution prior to this existence has been realized. They are therefore holders of a significant potential director, who should be put at the service of others, and not used for himself only. Few people can really use the potential of 11 and 22, because in general we use a mixture of two vibrations, namely 11/2 and 22/4, refer to the meaning of 2 and 4 for know more. The 22 is a powerful constructive energy, provided to use this energy universally, there too few people can really vibrate in 22.

At the relational level on the 11th and the 22nd, having a strong character, we often have difficulties with others. In a negative and ill-posed theme on the 11th and 22nd in some cases, psychic and / or physical imbalances, it is somehow enlightenment or madness, it is of course not systematic and fortunately. So when you meet an 11 or a 22 in a theme or both at the same time, study the good because they are rich in information.

Hoping that this book will bring you keys in understanding your karma.

Jean Marc Vignolo,

www.numerologueconseils.com

Printed in the USA
CPSIA information can be obtained
at www.ICGtesting.com
CBHW051306211123
2006CB00047B/807